HOW TO CHOOSE YOUR CHILD'S SCHOOL

ANTHONY EKANEM

Made with ♥ on the Notion Press Platform
www.notionpress.com

Contents

Preface   v

1. Schooling Basics   1

2. What Are Your Child's Needs?   2

3. Think About Your Educational Values   4

4. Research The School's Philosophy   6

5. Research Extra Curricula And Programs   8

6. Consider Your Finances   10

7. Visit The School   12

8. If The Child Is In The Wrong School   14

Preface

Having a good education is very important, as it will eventually contribute positively to a better life for the individual. Therefore, most parents take the trouble and time to search for the best school for their children to ensure a good start in life.

CHAPTER ONE

Schooling Basics

Some schools are known for their academic excellence while others may be noted for their excellent sporting programmes. The parent would have to decide which would be more suitable for their needs and those of the child in question.

If this decision proves to be a challenge at this stage, then finding a school which is competent in both areas would also be acceptable. Convenience would also usually be another point to look into as no parent wants their child to have to sit through a one-hour ride just to get to school and another one-hour ride to get home.

This is also important from an emergency angle where the parent would be able to reach the child's school within the shortest time possible. Taking the time to check up on the school by speaking to others who have children already attending the facility would also be another way to gauge the suitability of the school.

There is also the need to check the requirements, if any, that need to be met to be successfully admitted to the school.

CHAPTER TWO

What Are Your Child's Needs?

Finding out as much as possible about the schools within the suitable radius to fit the convenience of both child and parent would be a good start to choosing a school for the child. This should then be followed with more in-depth research as to what the schools identified can offer and how these will benefit the child in question.

There are several things to consider when it comes to the future of the child at the eventual choice made and the following are just some areas that should ideally be covered.

Perhaps the first would be to contact the local educational centres to find out about all the various schools within the ideal perimeter to suit the initial need to limit the distance between the school and the place of residence of the family.

Once the particular school has been identified, then the parent would have to make a more in-depth study as to the suitability and comforts it can provide for the child who is going to be enrolled.

Some children may need special attention for various reasons, and the school chosen should be able to cater for these needs adequately. The physical and mental comfort of the child at the school should ideally be an important factor when choosing the ideal school.

The services extended outside the actual study curriculum such as outdoor activities would also have to be considered if the child is particularly fond of the outdoors.

Some children need to have this kind of learning experience to ensure they are kept interested and stimulated by the idea of education.

Considering if the child will eventually be comfortable with the other children attending the school is also another element to be considered. Some children are simply not able to adjust well to other cultures and styles that are foreign to them.

CHAPTER THREE

Think About Your Educational Values

Almost everyone has some idea of the educational values they would like to see their children adopt. Researching the type of values the intended school follows would help to decide its suitability for both the parent and child.

The parent would have to first understand the particular value system they would like their children to be exposed to and then seek out the school using such a system.

The values of education can be connected to either the actual teachings at the school or to the methodology used for the imparting of knowledge to the children at the school.

Both these are very different value systems that should ideally be understood before the decision to enrol is made.

Here, the way and form the teachers impart the relevant curriculum outlines and content to the children would sometimes be a more important issue for the parent rather than what is being taught.

This is mainly because most of the educational materials would already be dictated by the governing educational body at the time, thus the concerns in that area would not be as pivotal to the parent decision in terms of enrolment.

The method chosen by the school and the teaching staff as a whole would certainly be of some concern to the parent as they would want the child to have a good learning experience throughout their tenure at the school.

Then there is the actual content that is being imparted in the form of education for the child eventually earmarked to attend the school chosen. For some parents, the content of the material to be taught would have to be in line with their belief systems thus creating an ideal extension of what the child is already taught at home.

CHAPTER FOUR

Research the School's Philosophy

Since the children will probably be in the school chosen throughout the tenure or phase of a particular period of educational needs, there should be some understanding of the school's philosophy and if it is suitable for both the child's needs and the parent's approval.

The school's philosophy should ideally be along the lines that would be approved by the parents intending to choose that particular school simply based on its perceived and touted philosophical elements.

Besides the long-term effect, it will have on the child attending the school, other connective issues would have to be considered, such as the overall costs, and eventually, the results the child is expected to be able to achieve with the school's help.

Ideally, the school's philosophy should be an extension of the family's value system as this will make it easier and less confusing for the child attending the school.

Ensuring the school follows closely all the various ideas it advertised to the potential parent making enquiries, is very important as in some cases the parent eventually notes that the school chosen for its philosophies does not follow what it initially promised.

Areas such as how the rules are enforced, what rules the school outlines, how the teaching staff tackles problems and problematic students, how the student are expected to simulate into the school environment, how the school encourages different cultures and beliefs into their system and many other equally important elements that will eventually impact the child's thought process in some way.

All the various philosophies can be explored by visiting the school in person and with the child or simply by talking to other families whose children attend the intended school of choice.

CHAPTER FIVE

Research Extra Curricula and Programs

Having a complete overall schooling or education experience is very important for the eventual growth of the child both mentally and physically.

Unfortunately for some, there is a growing trend to focus mainly on the educational needs of the child rather than the overall physical needs as well.

A healthy learning environment should also be able to encourage a good amount of physical activity to ensure the body and brain are adequately stimulated and alert to better cope with the educational materials the child is going to be expected to absorb.

Therefore it would be prudent to make the necessary inquiries as to the types of extra-curricular activities and programs that are actively offered at the school.

This will also help the parent avoid the need to source for such complimenting activities outside the school system. This would not only be very inconvenient but would also incur more cost and time for the parent.

For the child too, it would be rather inconvenient to seek such added element elsewhere and in most cases, people will eventually opt not to focus on these areas and thus lose out in the long run to activities that could have proven to be useful in one way or another.

Having the choice of a good number of extra-curricular activities and also varied programs will also give the child the opportunity to be exposed to other interesting beneficial elements other than just plain education. This is also important as this is often the best way to spot talent in a particular field that is not particularly educationally based.

CHAPTER SIX

Consider Your Finances

Providing a child with a good education will allow the child to have a good foundation that will lead to better prospects in life. With the emergence and popularity of the private sector going into providing education, more people are choosing to opt for this style of providing education for their children.

Choosing between the two styles of public and private schooling should not be done lightly as this is a long-term commitment and would ideally require some serious thought.

Deciding on the private schooling style can be very costly especially when a parent's earnings are no longer guaranteed. This will eventually affect the child's progress and growth in many ways should the initial option of private schooling would now have to be changed to public schooling due to the lack of funds.

It is sometimes very difficult for the child to adjust both mentally and academically as most private education styles are said to be more competitive and well-rounded in the curriculum content and execution. In the private schooling style, there is also a lot more attention given to the individual child's needs which is not forthcoming in the public school system.

This is mainly because there are a lot more children squeezed into one classroom environment, thus leaving the teacher little choice but to focus on those who are interested in learning. Therefore a child who is playful, inattentive or simply too lazy to focus on what is being taught, will simply be left behind.

However, if the focus is on providing the child with a good education, the parents should explore all types of private institutions and carefully work out the long-term costs it would involve educating the child in such a scenario.

CHAPTER SEVEN

Visit the School

When the child is reaching school going age, it would be the duty of the parent to start looking around for a suitable school for the child to attend. This should be done in a systematic manner that will ensure the most suitable and ideal educational environment is provided based on the choice made.

Part of the exercise of looking for a suitable school would be to talk to other parents whose children are attending the school intended, to get their views on the capabilities and other aspects of the school.

This is important as it will give the parent an actual account of the school and its background as opposed to simply reading about the school in published material.

A lot of materials written on the school and its capabilities are usually written in an advertising and promotional style thus leaving a lot of elements glazed over to appear attractive to the prospective parent.

After gaining as much information as possible on the school and deciding that it would probably be a good fit for the child, the next step would be to visit the school.

This will help the parent get a better feel for what is being offered and how the child will adapt to the new environment. It will also allow the parent to have a firsthand view of how things are done at the school.

Most schools especially the private ones will certainly go the extra mile to make the parent feel welcome and will promote the school as best as they can so that a good impression is made.

Those intending to visit a public school of their choice would also be able to do so without too much of a hassle.

CHAPTER EIGHT

If the Child is in the Wrong School

Most parents would ideally want their children to go to the best schools where the teaching and learning style is very competitive and good results are evident all year round.

However, the parent should also be aware that it is very important to choose a school that would most suit the individual child's needs and characteristics. This would be pivotal to the eventual complete rounded growth of the child both mentally and socially.

When a child is put into a school environment that is not suited to his or her capabilities, there could be some very detrimental effects that will eventually result in the child beginning to hate anything to do with education.

There are also a lot of cases where the child is very afraid to go to school, and this is usually caused by a variety of reasons, which range from an uninteresting curriculum to inadequate teaching tools.

There is also the possibility of not wanting to go to school because of bullying issues that are prevalent and not taken seriously by the school authorities thus causing a lot of problems for the physically weaker students.

Academically, if the child does not feel stimulated by the programs offered at the school, there would be the danger of boredom seeping in, and this too could create problems as the child seeks fulfilment elsewhere. This in most cases is of the negative kind, thus the importance of picking the right school for the child's future well-being.